HOW I SURVIVE THROUGH
THE GRACE OF GOD

HOW I SURVIVE THROUGH THE GRACE OF GOD

My Story of God's Grace

Elma L. Rivers

XULON PRESS

Xulon Press
2301 Lucien Way #415
Maitland, FL 32751
407.339.4217
www.xulonpress.com

Unless otherwise indicated, Scripture quotations taken from the New Revised Standard Version (NRSV). Copyright © 1989 the Division of Christian Education of the National Council of the Churches of Christ in the United States of America.

Edited by Xulon Press

Printed in the United States of America.

ISBN-13: 978-1-54566-885-6

Table of Contents

Introduction

A Reason for Hope

Dear readers, it is a miracle that I am able to share this story—my story—of God's grace with you. When I was a young mother at my lowest point, suffering emotional and verbal abuse and separated from my children, there was no hope in the natural sense that I would be anything significant in my life. The pain and obstacles seemed too great for me to overcome. But God has been faithful!

Through the challenges, the trials, the grief, and the heartaches, I learned that there was a God who cared about me *and* was more powerful than my troubles, and who wanted to use me to minister to others as well.

Maybe your life today seems like a hopeless story that will not have a happy ending. I assure you, even with all the miracles that God has done for me, from time to time I still have difficult days. Sometimes I forget God's faithfulness and I stumble a bit. But that in itself is a miracle also—that God is able to keep me on His path even though I am not perfect and I make many mistakes along the way.

Whatever the circumstances you are facing, I want you to know that God is bigger than any obstacle. His love is never-ending, and His grace is still making miracles today.

What He has done for me, He will do for you also. Your miracle story is just beginning.

> *To me, who am less than the least of all the saints, this grace was given, that I should preach... the unsearchable riches of Christ...* (Ephesians 3:20)

Chapter 1

My Early Days

*But by the grace of God I am what I
am, and His grace toward me was
not in vain; but I labored more abundantly than they all, yet not I, but
the grace of God which was with me.*
(I Corinthians 15:10)

My name is Elma Rivers. I was born Elma Lenora Lewis
on April 28, 1956, in Clare Valley Village, St. Vincent
and the Grenadines. Like many people who are born
into difficult family circumstances, I knew the pain
of separation early in my life. My parents separated
from each other when I was a couple of months old,
and in the aftermath of their relationship conflict, my
mother gave me to my father to raise. Though it may
seem uncommon for a child so young to be separated
from her mother, God still worked in my life and had
a plan to bless me despite anything that I would face
on my journey.

I was raised more by my paternal grandparents than by my father himself, as well as by my aunts and uncles who were very loving and caring towards me. My father belonged to a Spiritual Baptist Church, and though I spent much of my time with my grandparents, I went to my father's church every Sunday. This helped to instill in me the importance of faith and a relationship with God in my life.

One of the most formative things about my childhood was that my parents and grandparents taught me to pray when I had a problem, so I learned early in my life to go to God with my difficulties. This was a continual occurrence that would be part of my life for many years to come, even to the present day. Without this, I don't know where I would be today. It is one of the many ways that God has been gracious to me—it has been like a rudder to steer my ship through life's storms.

My grandparents especially were extremely nurturing and caring, and because of their role in my life, I had a wonderful childhood in my younger years. It is a time in my life that I look back on today with much gratefulness and thankfulness to God. Though the journey forward was not to be an easy one, this foundation would prove to be unshakable in future days.

When I was eight years old, my father got married to my stepmother, which brought some changes to our home. My stepmother was a lovely person who, though she had a few problems of her own, still tried her best to love as a mother. Life with her as part of our daily household went well—we occasionally had some family problems, as most families do from time to time, but it was a stable environment for me to grow up in as a child. Nevertheless, it still couldn't fill the longing in a child's heart for her true mother.

Years passed in my childhood and teenage life as I grew old enough to understand the good and the bad things that had formed my personal experiences. Though I wished my parents would not have separated, I grew accustomed to my life's circumstances and chose to make the best of them. In an effort to meld the various parts of my life together, I would go to see my mother as much as I could. When I would visit her she would show me love and care, touching that part of my heart that no one else could fill as she did.

I was eighteen years old and was living in Clare Valley Village, at that particular point in time, I cried a lot because I wanted to go and see my mother, then an opportunity arose to visit her. Through this visit to my mother changed my life forever. As a young girl, it was a bit rough not having that steady presence of her love and her touch to guide me through situations. This caused me to lean on God more, but it did not make the emotional aspect any easier.

This time that I went to see her, it came up in our discussion that a lady my mother knew of was interested in hiring someone to work with her in her home in Trinidad. After learning of this opportunity through my mother, I was drawn to it and I said I would go. I didn't have my passport in my possession, however, I went to the Fitz Hughes to my father because he had my passport. However, my father was opposed to the idea of my traveling and he hid the passport. It so happened, though, that my stepmother found the passport, and because of this I was able to get the opportunity to travel to Trinidad.

After all the arrangements had been made, I moved to Trinidad and worked with the lady for a year. This was to be the first of many jobs that I had that involved caring for children or working as a caregiver in people's homes. The lady was nice in her own way but I did encounter some difficulties there, especially with how she treated me.

I had been working for the lady for a year when I met my soon-to-be husband one night at the church I went to, which was not too far from where I worked. When I told him about the problems I was having, he urged me to leave the job, and one year later we were married. In retrospect, I don't think he truly loved me but I knew he cared for me. Rather, and he married me because of the challenges I was going through with the lady I worked for.

I was twenty years old when I got married. I had a lot to learn at that time about what love truly is, and I was not prepared for the heartbreak that would result from my marriage. Though my husband and I had children together, it did not solve the marriage difficulties that we experienced in those years. Now that I have lived longer and have a greater perspective on those years, I can see that it was a loveless marriage between the two of us. Although I'm sure we both had our faults, it seemed that everything had to be my husband's way — even minor things. Life was not easy. We had a lot of fights and the only reprieve we had of getting along without arguing seemed to be dependent on him having his own way.

We were living in a small house in Trinidad, a simple house that was nothing fancy but at least it was a place that was our own. To my surprise, my husband came home one day and informed me that he had decided we were going to move. Being pregnant with my second child, I was not eager to implement a lot of immediate change to our surroundings, especially since I didn't have a lot of trust in my husband.

My husband told me that he wanted to move to a different place in Trinidad, to a house that belonged to a certain older lady. His idea was that we would stay with her in her house and that one day, in the near future, we would be able to inherit the house. I didn't think it was a good idea, because we had a house of our own, though it was small. But my husband had made up his mind and he went ahead and sold our house.

When we moved to the older lady's home, my husband was always nice to the lady in hopes of eventually getting the house from her. It was not to be. Within a few years, I became pregnant with our third child there, but the change of where we were living and the soon arrival of another child did not alleviate the continuing marital problems that my husband and I experienced. When the strain of our relationship increased, he left us and we were separated from that moment on.

So many questions flooded my mind as a single mother. Was God truly good? What would happen to me and my children? How would I provide for them? What would I do next?

I had never imagined in coming to Trinidad that this would be what my life would look like within just a few years. Would I ever be able to get my life back together again?

Chapter 2

Starting Again

For by grace you have been saved through faith, and that not of yourselves; it is the gift of God, not of works, lest anyone should boast. (Ephesians 2:8-9)

When my husband left me, it would have been easy for me to completely run away from God. Now that I was all on my own in raising my children, I had to face the very strong temptation of not becoming anxious about how I would provide for all of us. I was six months pregnant and felt very much alone. But thank God, in the midst of the difficulties my heart remained open to what God could do for me.

One of the first things I did in starting again was to take my older son to live with his grandmother. This was not what I wanted for him, but I felt that I had no choice because of having to care for his younger brother with another baby on the way (who was to be my daughter).

The day after Christmas that year, I went to visit my son at his grandmother's home. At the time, I was not aware that my husband had gone to America when he left me. It was my mother-in-law, who told me that he went to America. Even though he and I were separated, I felt that I should have known this information because it very much affected us when I found out, I cried a lot, because I didn't know how I was going to make it. The international move by my husband seemed to make permanent what I had already suspected in my heart: he had no intention of coming back, which meant that I was on my own.

There I was, pregnant with my third child and painfully isolated—and the loneliness could be almost overwhelming at times because I had no family in Trinidad and Tobago. I was still a young lady and craved the stability that strong relationships can give. But I had love in my heart for God and I believed that he would make a way and that someone would come alongside me and help me. God was so good to me in my journey, in the midst of everything that happened. He provided for me in that trial—He sent help from His sanctuary!

One of the ways that God provided for me was just to keep us safe in our home. As a single mother especially, safety and well-being seemed to be dependent on my ability to protect myself, which could be unnerving at times. I remember one time I was sleeping in the house while pregnant, and I came to realize that a snake was living in the house. Talk about unsettling! But because God was with me, no snake ever bit me or my children.

God also provided for me financially to support my family. Two days after I learned that my husband had left for America, I got a job at Piarco International Airport. I knew it had to be God's intervention because business managers do not usually hire employees that are six months pregnant! God had given me the job at the airport so that I could support my family. It was a good-paying job, and I was so thankful to God for providing this answer to prayer for my family.

I also experienced God's provision in the form of a few good friends who helped me. My friend Helen took my second son so that I could work full shifts at my job and try to save up enough money so that after I had the baby I could survive as a single mother for three months until I could work again.

Finally, the time came to have the baby. In order to deliver my daughter, because I didn't have any family nearby I had to take a taxi to the hospital, which was very hard to do all by myself. My older son was with his grandmother, and my second son was with my friend so that I could go to the hospital to have the baby. Again I wrestled to fight away the feelings of deep loneliness that threatened to overtake me.

Through the struggles and the difficulties, I named my baby girl Victoria, because I had been victorious in all that God had provided for me. Despite the sense of loneliness that often loomed in my mind, God had been so good to me, and I had food, clothes, and everything I needed for my new baby. After I had given birth, I went to my friend's house to pick up my son, then I went home with him and the baby, and in a few months, I went back to work.

When my daughter was born, in addition to having no family in Trinidad, I also did not have a church family yet at that time. My saving grace through all of this was that I had learned from my grandparents to pray, and this carried me through difficult times. I would pray to God, and He would provide for me by sending the help I needed.

I had given birth to two of my children only ten months and two weeks apart—this was how old my second son was when my daughter was born, and my older son was only turning four years old. It was very hard not being able to have steady, ongoing help during that time, but God was so good, that anytime I had to go somewhere, He would send someone to me. Even sometimes when I was out on the street, people would give me rides to get to my destinations.

I had been in this situation a long time, but when I met a man named Richard, things changed a lot over the months that followed. One of the most significant changes was that Richard helped me frequently with the kids. I had met him through his mother when I was pregnant with Victoria, and I explained from the beginning that I couldn't be in a relationship at that point in my life. But he was very kind and respected me as I was still married, though I was separated from my husband. Even though I was unable to be in a relationship, Richard's friendship and support made it possible for me to handle the weight of being a single mother.

With Richard's help, I moved to the Belmont area. Richard had rented an apartment at Belmont and I was able to stay there and get back to work. This was part of God's provision for me so that my baby girl always had more than enough. Sometimes if Richard didn't have to go to work, he would take care of the children while I went to my job. Other times I would get a babysitter, who would come and take care of the children at the house so that I could work.

However, there were still challenges with balancing everything in my life. If the babysitter couldn't come (which happened more often than I hoped), I had to miss days at work and stay with the children, because I couldn't leave them by themselves. After all, I had two babies, so I had to take them somewhere. In the end, it was about three years total that I was on my own like this with the children.

Chapter 3

Making It Through

Let us then approach God's throne of grace with confidence, so that we may receive mercy and find grace to help us in our time of need. (Hebrews 4:16, NIV)

I was in a time of need. I was 25 years old and a single mother, it sometimes felt like mere survival rather than truly *living*. My children were very young and could not fully comprehend all that was happening in our lives, and it was probably better that way.

In the midst of the stress and strain, I often wondered how I was going to make it, but God was with me, and I cried out to Him often, asking for His help and His grace to carry me. He answered and continually supplied my needs despite the difficult circumstances in which I found myself.

In the course of events that took place during that season, my boss decided to open a business closer to where I was living in Belmont. He really wanted to help me, as he knew about my unique and challenging situation, and he offered for me to transfer to this new location, which was closer to home. Even though his moral support did make a felt difference in my life at that time, I still had the problem of not always being able to show up to work during my scheduled shifts.

Trying desperately for a solution before it was too late, I took all my children to their grandmother and told her I really needed her to help me with the children because I was having a hard time keeping my job. I left the children with her that day but she didn't want them to stay indefinitely, so I knew that it was not going to last and I needed a better answer for my predicament.

Eventually, my children's grandmother had someone come to me and asked me to come and pick up the children. When I took my children home, I realized the impact that my absence had on them. Most significantly, my daughter was having a noticeable problem with her mouth. I took her to the doctor to get help, but I felt partially to blame for her condition because I had been gone a lot and had not taken care of my daughter the way that I would have liked to.

One day, like a ticking time bomb, my boss finally warned me about my pattern of work absences. He said that because of how many days I had missed if the problem continued as it had been they would have to fire me. Unfortunately, that is exactly what happened, soon afterwards I lost my job.

Thankfully, before much time elapsed, I was able to acquire another job as a security guard. This meant that I had to leave my children at night to go to work, but God was still so good to me. Often I would ask my neighbor to help with the children, and God made a way so that I could come to attend to my children multiple times during the night and my employer never called me about it. Going back and forth from my job as a guard would normally have been a problem for my job performance, but God gave me favor to help me make it through.

The security guard job lasted a little while before things got hard. With my erratic schedule, the job eventually came to an end because my supervisors finally realized that I wasn't doing my job adequately. One night they came and I wasn't at my post, and when they asked me about it, I told them I was in the bathroom. They did not fire me that day, but they moved me to another location instead.

After one of my work shifts at the new location, I was on my way home when someone tried to mug me on the street. They tried to put me in their getaway car but I was able to escape. I went to the police station to report what had happened. After that scary incident, I knew that it wasn't safe for me to work that shift any longer, but the company didn't have another shift to offer me, and so the job came promptly to an end.

In the days that followed with yet another job hunt, things became even harder for us. One friend who would help with babysitting the children was not nice to them. One day, when a quarrel occurred between her children and mine, she poured a bucket of cold water on my children and I was very upset about what happened. I called the police because I didn't want to fight with her about it but I was very concerned about the safety of my children.

Shortly thereafter, I called my mother and asked her if she could help me with my kids. I reasoned that if I could get some help with care for them, I would have the chance to get on my feet again. Unfortunately, my mother said that she wouldn't be able to help me, so things continued to become very grueling emotionally for me.

I felt at that moment that I had exhausted all the options that I could think of in my constant brainstorming. More desperate with each day that passed, there were very few scenarios that I was not willing to consider. But there were certain lines that I knew I could not cross. I was a young woman who never did anything wrong with my body and I loved God—I just needed some help so that I could get a good job to support my family.

At that time I remembered that I had met a lady named Ms. Marie who was willing to help me with the children, and I went to her. She said that she would help me with the children so that I could get another job and go back to work. Ms. Marie offered for me to bring the children to her on Monday and pick them up at the end of the week. This was a significant opportunity for me so that I would not have to go home in the night to check on the children, and this lady was very good to all of us. But then came a time when she couldn't take the children any more, and so I had to go back to my ever-thinning list of possibilities.

In the period that I was seeking another job, I tried to make a special effort every weekend to spend the days with my kids and do special activities with them. I knew that this trying season had to be affecting them negatively, so I did my best to minimize the hardships for them (though I was very limited in what I could do). My heart wanted something so much better for them.

Then, all of a sudden, my husband came back from America. I had no idea that he had returned or even that he had plans to do so any time soon. I was picking up my older son from his grandparents' house for Christmas and New Year holidays as I normally did, and much to my surprise, my husband was there.

He had not even come to look for the children—so there was clearly no intention on his part to work on resolving our marriage. When he eventually came to his mother's home, I told him about my situation and what had happened, and I told him, "I love my children and I want what is best for them." I asked him, "Can you help my children come to America so they can have a better life than what I can give them?"

At the time, I was living in my own apartment taking care of my kids. Somehow, through our short conversation, my husband decided that he would take care of the kids—he would send money to support them. So he started sending the funds to his mother for the children. Along with the funds, he decided to begin filing the papers for them to travel to America.

As these developments took place, on one occasion in the summertime the kids were spending time with his family. I called to talk to my children, and the family told me that my husband had paid for the children to come to America and that he would be going to the American embassy to finalize the arrangements. But this step had taken place without my awareness, so it appeared that he was planning to take our children without my knowledge or involvement.

So my children did come to America when my daughter was about eight and my oldest son about eleven. My husband paid for them to come to America,

17

and they came legally through a green card. I, however, didn't come at that time.

It was a devastating experience to be separated from my children, but still, God worked through everything for our good. Many times since then I have thought of the Bible verse Romans 8:28, which says: "And we know that in all things God works for the good of those who love Him, who have been called according to His purpose" (NIV).

I knew that God had called me to believe in Him, to love Him, and to be His servant. In just a few brief words, this verse from Romans already at that time encapsulated my life testimony in my walk with God.

Living completely separated from my children for the first time in my life, I would pray for my children daily and I would regularly write letters to them, hoping that my messages would reach them. It ended up being like this for a couple of years. Little did I know that I actually would have the opportunity to come to America myself and be closer to my children. That was soon to become one of the greatest expressions of God's grace that I had yet seen.

Chapter 4

Weaving of Grace

*And of His fullness we have all received,
and grace for grace.* (John 1:16)

The circumstances of my coming to America were far from a fairy tale or the perfect dream. It certainly wasn't the story I would have written for myself if it were up to me. But as a tapestry is woven, often feeling stretched and pulled and looking extremely disheveled on the side where the work is being done, the process nevertheless is creating a final work of beauty on the other side once the artist's vision is realized. I am grateful that my God the great Artist was at work in my circumstances to bring about His plan of blessings for us.

The events surrounding my move came to be through meeting another man in Trinidad, with whom I had two additional children. In the sense of providing for the children, he was a very good father who took care of their needs. But he was very abusive verbally and physically. So although he did provide for the family, it was not a safe place for us to live, and I still carried a longing within me for true fulfillment in my life. Sadly, this man would verbally and physically abuse me—if I said anything that upset him. It was a terrible reality for all of us.

On one occasion during that period of time, my husband came back from America and he brought my oldest son with him, to visit me. But the man with whom I was living didn't want my son to come to his house, so I prayed and prayed and asked God to make a way for me to navigate through this situation.

God works in mysterious ways! Unexpectedly, with the help of a friend of mine whom God used to give me favor, I was able to say to the man I was with that I would like to go to America to visit my other children. To my amazement, he went to the embassy to get the visas for us. The first part of the breakthrough had happened, and I was shocked.

I was not able to come to America immediately after getting my visa, because my fourth child had a major exam and I needed to stay in Trinidad during that time. So I had to wait a bit longer. The days turned into months which turned into a few years, but the favor God had given me was making a way. The table was being set, and it was only a matter of time before my traveling became possible.

A couple of years after I got the visa, I was still with the second man in Trinidad. He had an excellent job with a wealth of finances that provided well for the family. (One of the major blessings that came from being with him was that we never needed anything—because it was provided for.) With the way his job was structured, in one instance, in particular, he benefited from some additional money when he received a back pay. To sum up in brief what happened, he gave me some money to come to America, though he did not come to America himself. Amazingly, God used the difficult life's circumstances to win my second partner's favor so that I could get free of that abusive environment and begin again in America.

When I was in Trinidad with this man, he didn't want to marry me. I couldn't live that life anymore and that was the primary reason that I left him, too, after having been left by my husband. So I departed from Trinidad and began searching for a new life in America. This search for belonging led me to become a Jehovah's Witness when I came to America. I was baptized as a Jehovah's Witness, and on the weekends I would go with them to evangelize and preach to others. It was not until later that I realized that God had something better for me than what I experienced in that religious community.

Coming to America

Upon coming to America, I was able to reunite with my other children for regular visits, and sometimes they would come to stay with me on the weekends. The circumstances were such that my first husband lived in New Jersey, and I lived in Brooklyn, New York.

Today my children are grown and have their own families, and I have grandchildren through them that have brought great joy to my life!

In America, I first stayed with my friend Joanne, who picked me up at the airport and let me stay with her for a while until I got a job. The result of my searching was that I got a babysitting job in North Carolina. But it was a difficult time for me. Some ongoing problems soon surfaced for me, because each time I held the baby, it reminded me of my baby I left behind in Trinidad. I missed them very much, and this caused me to cry a lot and became depressed. So I came back to New York to seek some professional help.

When I came back, however, my friend no longer had the space, someone else was living there. So, I went to stay in Queens, New York with my father who, when I asked, said that I could stay with him.

Once I secured my temporary housing with my father, I went to seek help in group meetings where we could talk and process through the painful things we had experienced. Most of the people had the same types of problems as I did, and I came to a much better place of personal well-being because I got the help.

With my feet back under me emotionally and physically, I got a job in Queens. One day, however, while staying at my father's house, my brother and I had a misunderstanding and we exchanged some heated words with each other. Although my father didn't hear what my brother had said to me, my father *did* hear something that I said to my brother and he put me out on the streets again, in the winter. He had put me out when I was fifteen years old, and now he was doing it again.

Upset by the situation, I managed to make some friends who lived in the same apartment building, as I reached out for someone—anyone—who could help. Among these new friends were a married couple, Chad and Rose, whom I asked if I could stay with them, and they said yes. So at least it was a short-term solution, but I still felt uncomfortable, because I felt that it would be best for me to have at minimum a small place for myself.

A Place to Live

One day, providentially, I stayed home from work and I went to the laundromat, where I saw a sign that said, "Room for rent". So I called the lady who owned the place and I told her I was looking for a room—but I also shared the truth with her that I didn't have the money to pay for it. Still, she said to come and talk with her, and she said I could move into the room without the money, giving me permission to take some more time and pay her when I had the money. This was a circumstance in which God showed me such grace and favor and so beautifully provided for me.

On top of this favor, I had just experienced, I was in for another surprise. As I was leaving the building where my father and friends lived to move into my new room, I didn't have any furniture at all to move in with to get myself set up there. On my way walking to the new place, I met a lady and I told her I was moving into a room, and she gave me a whole bedroom set of furniture—including a bed and a dresser so that I could get started in my new place. By the time I moved into the room, it was already furnished! God had provided a room of my own for me, and He even miraculously provided the furnishings to set it up comfortably. What a gracious God we serve!

The owners of the new place where I was staying were very nice people, so much so that one time when I was sick they took care of me. I lived there for about three years with them, then the woman's son who was in college wanted to come back, so she wanted to have the room again and I had to move out.

Following this change in circumstance, I went and I got an apartment in East New York. Unfortunately, this did not last long as the job in Queens came to an end. Instead, I got a job in Pennsylvania to take care of two children for a nice family. Someone told me about an apartment that was available near my new job location, and I went to see it in Philadelphia. It was a one-bedroom place and I decided to take it.

As I started the job in Philadelphia, I was earning $400 per week, and the people were extremely nice there. I would sometimes stay with them for extended periods and just come home to my apartment every two weeks. The only problem with the apartment was that I would hear gunshots in that area, and I only lived there for about four months after I began staying for two weeks at a time with the family that I worked for.

One day as I came home from my job, I discovered that someone had broken into the apartment and had taken all of the large items out of my living space. After I saw what had happened, I remembered that it was the grace of God that had gotten me this far. I had been through so much already, but God had always shown Himself true. Still, I didn't feel safe staying there any longer.

I left Philadelphia and returned to New York, thankfully, I was able to go back and stay for a little while with the people I had lived with after my father had put me out of his house. During that time I worked Monday to Thursday cleaning apartments, and then I would sell souse on the weekends in a small business of my own to make some additional money. The owners of the place didn't make me pay any money to stay there this time, but I would give them some money out of my earnings anyway because they were so good to me. Because of the favor, I found with them, I could even cook there in their house and use more time to focus on selling the items that I made to earn a profit. On the weekends I would go elsewhere, both to give them their space and also to devote time to go to Church and my small business. God was so good to me, and I was so thankful!

Working in Florida

During that time someone told me about a promising job in Florida, and I decided to go there to pursue the opportunity because I wanted to have a house of my own—a real home—one day. I thought to myself that if I would work and save money, I could accomplish this dream of mine. So I went to Florida to live, leaving my friends, though I stayed in contact with them.

In Florida, I worked in a home taking care of the elderly. I would work during the day, and I decided I would sign up to take some classes in the evenings. Having come to Florida, I knew that I needed to put in some effort to improve my life situation. That way, I reasoned, if I needed to go back to New York, I could prepare myself to do something better than I had previously done when I lived in New York.

Like me, one girl that I worked with at my job was also part of the Jehovah's Witnesses. I had signed up to take classes on Tuesday and Thursday each week, but the girl at my job wanted me to cover her work shifts on those days, supposedly so that she could go to the Jehovah's Witnesses meetings. But I think she was just trying to use me because we all are responsible for our salvation in the Lord. I felt that she was just pretending to make the spiritual reason the basis for her request.

I did not want to do what my co-worker had asked, because I had signed up for the classes at school and I felt that this should be my priority. This resulted in my boss terminating my job because she thought I should have fulfilled the request for the girl. When this happened, I no longer had any reason to stay in Florida.

After that instance and other smaller but similar occurrences, I began to disconnect myself from the Jehovah's Witnesses community. For example, one strange pattern was when I went to the Kingdom Hall meeting place, someone who was also involved would give me a ride, but I wasn't free to go to the school instead if I chose to do so. The people who were part of that community were trying to tell me what I could and couldn't do, which made me feel very uneasy. So I escaped from that life and I went back up to New York.

Back Again in New York

In New York once again, now free from that unhealthy spiritual environment, my search for God's path for my life continued. I stayed with a friend at first for a little bit, and then I went and rented my own room. The lady that I was staying with was nice to me, but I was starting to feel like it was time for me to have my own apartment. I went and rented a kitchenette for myself, and then soon afterwards I went to look for an apartment to rent.

I prayed and asked God to show me the place He had for me, because I had seen His goodness and grace in the past, and I believed that He had something special that He wanted to do in my life. So one day I said very intently, "God, I would like to get my own apartment—show me where the right place is and please help me to get it. Help me to be in the right place at the right time."

At the time I was working as a babysitter four days a week, and then I got another job for the weekends. One weekend I was going to work, and I happened to see a certain lady whom I asked if she knew anyone who owned an apartment, and she said yes. So she gave me the lady's name and number, and I went to see the apartment that I am still living in to this day.

In all these things and many seasons, God has provided for me. I have had misfortunes, yes, and many times things did not turn out the way I expected—but I'm still alive! And I have to count all my joy because of God's overflowing grace towards me. Only He could take the challenging circumstances of my life and weave together a beautiful story out of those difficulties and disappointments. Not only did He do this for me, but He also began to open up opportunities so that I could share with others what He had done—and tell them that He could do the same for them.

Chapter 5

A True Friend

*As each one has received a gift, minister
it to one another, as good stewards of
the manifold grace of God.* (I Peter 4:10)

The new apartment that I moved into was the best one
that I have lived in so far. Surrounding the house in
the immediate neighborhood were a lot of wealthy
people who lived near me, and I was able to furnish
my house with very nice items that I got from my job.
I was grateful for the new place and for the blessings
that came along with it, many of which was a brand new
type of experience for me.

Despite the blessing that the new apartment was,
however, the greatest blessing that I received during that
time was not the comfort of a sizable apartment or the
benefits of living in an upscale neighborhood—instead,
it was the priceless treasure of a true and faithful friend.

Mrs. Melderson was an elderly lady whom I met
while working at my job as a babysitter, and whom I
began to work for also as a part-time caregiver in her

home. She was a Jewish lady with a warm personality and a sweet spirit, who was always considerate towards me and ready with a kind word. She taught me so much about life, and I was eager to learn as much as I could from her. In her signature caring way, she taught me about so many practical, everyday things, and I often talked to her about God and my faith in Him.

Mrs. Melderson had another lady who worked for her at that time—an American, who seemed neither to enjoy her work nor to be motivated by it. For my part, I loved to work; I went to my job and tried to do my best. In my view, I simply did what I needed to do. I was naturally accustomed to this perspective—it was part of my personality and part of my faith.

The fundamental difference between the other caregiver and me caused her to feel threatened by me. The circumstance that particularly provoked this situation was that she worked Mondays to Fridays and I worked on the weekends. Sometimes, though she worked five days a week, she would leave almost all the work for me to do. But I didn't mind, because Mrs. Melderson was always nice and understanding; so when I went to work, I loved to do my best.

Nevertheless, I wanted to make sure that Mrs. Melderson understood what was happening. So I went to her one day and I explained the situation about the lady who worked for her. As we talked about it, there wasn't much that we needed to do. The reason was that the two of us shared a very similar perspective, and from that day on, there was an unspoken understanding between Mrs. Melderson and myself. She grew to love me and I loved her like a grandmother, as she reminded me of my grandmother. I continued to talk with her often when I went to work there. As the days passed and I became a mainstay working in her home, I always had a lot of favor with her.

You would never know it by looking at Mrs. Melderson, but she was a Holocaust survivor who had lost her mother and family in that tragic event of hor-rific violence against the Jews. Because she was well acquainted with hardship of her own, I felt very com-fortable sharing with her about my life story and the challenges I had faced (and was still facing). She would listen to me with a sense of quiet knowing in her eyes as I recounted the valleys I had walked through with my children and past relationships. I shared my journey of continually having to find places to live and to work to support my family, of the difficulties surrounding my circumstances, and how God still was taking care of me and guiding me.

Though my trials did not rival hers from her past, the mutual experience that the two of us shared of feeling alone in the midst of personal suffering united our hearts in a unique bond—it was a profound aspect of life that we had in common.

One time, as the school year was beginning, I wanted to send a package to my two children who were still in Trinidad, but I didn't have the money to do it. I went to Mrs. Melderson house to work that day and was talking to her, and I explained that their school year was beginning and I didn't have the money to send the items to my children. At that very moment, she decided to give me the money that I needed. I was very grateful but I didn't want to just take the money from her, so as soon as she gave it to me, I decided I was going to pay her back and treat it as a loan. I have always believed that even if someone is nice to you, you shouldn't take advantage of the situation. Especially in the case of my friendship with Mrs. Melderson, her friendship meant a lot to me and the last thing that I wanted to do was to take this special gift for granted.

The two of us shared a very special connection, even about things that would seem at first to be small and insignificant. For instance, sometimes if I wanted to go shopping, I would take the sales catalog to her. I would tell her that I wanted to buy an item, and she would say to me, "Don't buy it—there is going to be a sale next week!" This was just one example of how she became just like my grandmother to me.

Mrs. Melderson taught me so many things that I didn't know, such as how to buy nice clothes. She would always say to me, "Elma, don't buy too many cheap clothes!" She taught me that I should have one good dress and make sure that it is of good quality (including which manufacturer names were the best to buy), and to buy other pieces in my wardrobe that were not as fancy but would last a long time. She educated me about what I should and shouldn't buy—not just with clothes, but with everything. All the things that she passed on to me made me the confident person that I am today. She was the greatest role model in my life in that part of my journey.

I continued in my job and friendship with her until she died, about five years after I met her. I was so committed to this lady that I took it upon myself to always be looking out for her. Sometimes I would go to the job and I would see that the other lady who worked for her didn't cook, but instead would just prepare a meal from a can. In my culture, we didn't eat canned food frequently—especially not when it came to preparing a meal for the elderly. When I went to her on weekends, she would often be sick and wouldn't be up for talking when I arrived. So I would ask her for money to go to the store and purchase groceries, then I would prepare chicken soup, split pea soup or lentil soup for her, and she would begin to talk again.

So "my old lady," as I call her, grew to love me because I treated her as if she were my grandmother. My motto was that "I treated her how I would want to be treated." After I prepared some nice food, I would put it in containers for her, and I would tell the other lady to give it to her throughout the week. I said to the other lady, "You have to take care of your patient—this is your patient!"

I told Mrs. Melderson that I was giving her my commitment that I would stay with her no matter what, until the end. I knew that at her age, her ability to take care of herself would most likely only decrease even further with time. Sometimes when she would be sick, I would have to stay over with her on the job. And when I stayed over with her, I would sleep in the same bedroom. Because she was a Jewish lady, she already was set up with two beds in her room, which made the sleeping arrangement easy to facilitate. When staying overnight, I would stay in the same room, so I would know right away if something happened to her in the middle of the night. This was how she knew that I loved her and that I would care for her regardless of the circumstance as I would care for my children or my mother. She was the same as family to me.

She had a special way of caring for me also like a daughter or granddaughter. Despite her elderly physical condition, whenever I left her place and came to my home, she would worry about *me* and would call at least twice a week to see how I was doing! Because I often would share with her some of my story during our visits, it caused us to have a deeper relationship.

Mrs. Melderson even had a direct interest in and concern for my personal relationships. Because I was a Christian, I already believed that if I met a man, I couldn't live with him without being married. It was my conviction that I couldn't just have a boyfriend and share an apartment with him because it would be adultery; so I always made it my goal to live righteously in every way. But Mrs. Melderson took it to another level of safety. If I met a man, she would tell me to bring him to her house so that she could meet him and help me to make a wise decision about him. That was how close we had gotten to each other. She would talk to the guy, and if she had a concern then she would say to me, "Elma, no no! He's no good!"

Our close relationship meant that when the other caregiver went on vacation, I would work for my old lady the whole week. During that season of my life, I also would decline other potential job offers. Once when I received a job opportunity to work in Westchester, New York, I didn't take the job because I had made the long-term commitment to Mrs. Melderson, and I told myself that if I left, she would die from lack of care. So I stayed with her to the end.

Through the course of my ever-deepening relationship with her, God was teaching me how to talk with her in a loving way about Him. Sometimes I would tell her how much God had done for me. I had a passion for this, and I frequently would talk with her about God on the weekends that I spent with her. As is often the case for many people, this is the most effective way to tell them about who God is—your personal testimony of what God has done for you. She would ask me, "Why do you work so hard, Elma?" So one day I took the opportunity to tell her that the job I worked Monday to Friday didn't pay a lot and that I had to work on the weekends so that I would have enough money. And I said, "I thank God for this job, because God provided this job for me."

I was thankful for every day that I got to spend with Mrs. Melderson, because I didn't know how long I would still have her with me. I just trusted that God was using me to be an encouragement and strength to her in the final season of her life. She was feeling very sick, so I was praying and asking God to help me and give me wisdom, knowledge, and understanding about how to talk to her about Him, so that if something would happen to her, she could enter into God's everlasting Kingdom. I kept asking God for an opportunity to share with her before she passed away.

In what turned out to be the last week that I went to work for her, I spoke with her about God's love and how good God is. I wasn't sure how much she was embracing what I was saying to her, but in the end she did reach out to Jesus in a personal way before she died. In one of her final moments, I prayed with her. I said, "Jesus Christ died so that we could have for-giveness from our sins." Right then, she said the name "Jesus" three times. I rejoiced that God had opened her heart and that in her own way she had reached out in faith to Him.

Besides my relationship with God which was always with me, I saw through my relationship with Mrs. Melderson that at least I had found one good friend whose memory would always be with me as well. When she died, I was sad beyond words and missed her more than I could have imagined. Sometimes I still miss her, though it has been several years since that time. I am still in touch with her children and have an ongoing relationship with them. I regularly call them to see how they are doing, and when I do so I always look for an opportunity to share God's love with them as I did with their mother.

My friendship with Mrs. Melderson showed me that no one is beyond God's ability to reach him or her, and that all He needs is an ordinary person who is available to Him—someone with a simple willingness to stretch out his or her hands to a neighbor who needs to know Him personally. Though I often didn't know what to say or when to say it in my relationship with her, I learned how to truly love her first and then God opened the door for her to receive His love through the words I shared with her. Through that experience, my life was forever changed. It has become one of the most fulfilling things in my life to daily ask God to use me to share His love with those who need it—no matter how young or how old they may be.

Chapter 6

Planting for the Future

By the grace God has given me, I laid a foundation... (I Corinthians 3:10)

When Mrs. Melderson passed away, I realized that a new and different season was upon me. My heart would always remember her, and yet I knew that God would have other assignments for me to fulfill in the coming days.

It was a bittersweet time, but in the midst of the changes, I continued to remain close to her family, especially to one of her daughters but also to all her children. This much I knew would not change even though the circumstances were now different.

I knew that God wanted to give me direction for the future, so I made it a matter of praying frequently. As I would see soon, the days were coming when He would make a way for me to put down more permanent roots in my life in America.

In the immediate time following Mrs. Melderson's passing, I still had my prior babysitting job that I would work from Monday to Friday, but I didn't have a weekend job for a little while because I was no longer working for her. I phased through a lot of different jobs over time.

For a brief stint, I found a new babysitting job in Queens, but then the family moved to New Jersey. Following this I worked with a man from Jamaica who did construction; that was a unique experience for me! As he worked in the building, I would clean the areas of the building and I would also spackle and plaster the walls. After that, I worked to pick up a child after school five days a week, and then I cleaned apartments and the list goes on. I had a lot of different jobs here and there to keep me afloat. Many types of employment helped me to keep a roof over my head during that time and were not necessarily permanent jobs.

After six years of being in America and continuing to work on a temporary basis without my green card, I met a lady on the train and she offered me a job to work as a court clerk. But I didn't have my green card, so I couldn't get the job. Through circumstances such as these, I was starting to realize that I needed to make that step of permanent residence soon in order to be able to capitalize on any new job opportunities that I may find as I continued in my employment search.

One Sunday afternoon I finally came to a decision that I needed to go get my green card, in order for me to get a solid job in America. With that decision, I began the process of applying for permanent residence. It was a struggle for me, but having seen how far God had brought me I trusted that He would work everything out the way that it needed to be.

The first person I turned to for help was my oldest son. I asked him to assist me with the application, he said yes. The issue of permanent residence was something I would come to in time; for the moment, however, I just knew that not having my green card was not the best situation for me, and I was looking for help to get started in that direction.

Unfortunately, not everyone in my family was supportive of the idea. One day, I went to my father and asked him to assist me in getting my green card by filing a Petition on my behalf. But he told me outright, "No!", and I was devastated, I cried and cried. Ever since I was a child, whenever I needed something I would ask him for it and he would give it to me. It was a shock to my system that he did not want to support me in this very important step.

I was so upset by his reaction to me, that God even used a complete stranger to comfort me. I met a man on the street whose name was Randy, who had seen me crying because of the situation. He told me not to worry. I was still very devastated, about the interaction with my father. I went to my prayer time and I said, "God, I know that everything happens in this life for a reason." So I managed to jump up again and kept going, hoping for the best—but it took me a couple of days to recover.

I still didn't have the answer as to how I was going to complete the process successfully. I told God that I wasn't going to marry someone just to be able to get my permanent residency in America. I knew that to be married again it had to be with someone I loved, and for the right reasons—based on building a relationship that was going to last. So although I thought about it, I did not seek to get married in that season of time.

After talking to my son to try to get some ideas about how to move forward, I took a lot of steps to improve my standing to be able to get a job. In the meantime, I also completed many of the requirements for my green card. But without my green card, I was limited in how I could move forward in my life. So I decided I would wait for my son to help me with the process and not to try to get my green card through other methods such as marriage.

Then, however, a major interruption in the process happened. My son called and said he was being sent to Iraq in his military position, and asked me to pray so he wouldn't have to go. All of a sudden, the green card took a back seat, because I was very worried and devastated about the possibility of my son being deployed to Iraq. At that time and even to this day, I go to church sometimes during the week where I have the opportunity to pray with others. So I brought the prayer request that night to the prayer meeting — so that my son wouldn't have to be deployed to Iraq.

In the end, thanks to the prayers and to God's grace over my son, God worked it out so that he did not have to go to Iraq, which I was extremely thankful for. My son called and he told me that many of the soldiers in his same division had died or suffered injuries while deployed, so I told him, "God protected you."

Finally, everything worked out and I got in touch with my son and we decided to hire a lawyer, who completed the application for my green card and submitted it. We then had problems with the application, because of the way he filled out the paperwork did not ensure the most efficient process.

One day I realized it had been a long time and I had not heard from the immigration department, and the Spirit of God prompted me to check the status on the internet. So I called my son and asked if he could check it for me because I did not have internet access in those days. My son said he was very busy, but I had a young female friend who was able to check the status of the application on the internet for me instead. When she checked the status of my application, it said: "Denied". This was due to the issues with my lawyer, who was not submitting my paperwork in a timely manner, and I found out that they still needed medical documentation from me, among other things. So then when this happened, I started getting worried that the immigration department was going to deport me.

But I didn't give up. I took the circumstance and the results to prayer, and I said, "God, there must be a way! Show me what to do!" I went to prayer because I didn't know what else to do at that moment. As so often happens in our lives, God's answer came in a way that I would least expect it to come.

I was going to a job one weekend, a place where a friend of mine usually worked. That weekend she had given me the opportunity to work in her place, from Friday night to Sunday night. After she called me and gave the address, I started out towards the location to begin my shift.

When I arrived there, I met a lady whose birthday I learned was in July, and I felt the Spirit of God telling me to bless her by giving her some money. I didn't know how I would do that, but I felt that God had spoken to me. So I decided that I would give her $100 to bless her, and the two of us became friends.

My new friend got me a very nice job that was paying $900 per week. Having become such good friends with each other, one day she asked me, "Do you have your green card?" I recounted to her how I had been denied when I applied for it. She probed me further, asking what exactly had happened, and I told her that I received the letter saying I was denied, I didn't know why, and that I couldn't get in touch with my son, because he was working out of town and didn't have good cellular service where he was.

My friend responded that she would call the lawyer who had arranged for her green card, and when she did I got an appointment for the next day with him. So I went and gave him all my information so he can start working on my case. There was a fee for his services, but I didn't have the money at the time, so my friend paid the lawyer's fee on my behalf. When I got paid, I paid her back. Through it all, I learned from this series of events to listen closely to the voice of God—that when God tells you to do something, you need to do it! It is because He has a reason behind His commands that He tells us to do certain things.

After we had paid for the lawyer's services, he got in touch with my son and after a couple of months, I was able to get my green card. Praise the Lord! For His, Mercies endures forever, His answer to prayers! Shortly thereafter, I went for an interview to finalize the process of getting a new job, now that my green card had come.

As soon as I had my green card, I started to work "on the books" legitimately for taxation and within all the legal parameters of permanent residency. I didn't want to work "off the books" any longer now that I had the appropriate legal status to be able to both reside and work permanently in the United States, to pay taxes, and also to start paying into my Social Security for the future. I felt such a relief and a new settledness in my life to now be planted for the future in a greater way.

I couldn't go to school right away at that time—I did manage to take some classes sporadically, but it didn't fully work out for me to be a student just yet. I had previous bills to pay that was already past due, and I felt that I was in a season personally in which I needed to focus on getting everything in my life financially sound. I believed in giving both my tithes and also extra offerings to God, in paying my bills, and in taking responsibility financially for everything else that was part of my life.

I started on my new job and I worked there for a couple of months to get more established with a steady income. After I had paid off a couple of my outstanding bills, I went to school for a while, and then I signed up with an employment agency and I started working again.

Having my green card in my possession, it was a relief to work "on the books"—and though everything is a roller-coaster when putting down roots in a new country, I could feel some much-needed solidity coming into my life.

When I was in other working situations in the past, I did have the stability of a "real" full-time job, working seven days a week and the money was deposited directly into the bank. I would write the check from that account each month to the landlord to pay my rent. But when I came to New York to also go to school in addition to working, I wasn't putting in full-time hours yet at my job because I had to work my way up to that status with the employer. Until such a scenario would come to pass, I found a way to cover my bills so that I didn't have any problem.

But now things were different. This time I had the opportunity to enter into the stability of more permanent employment from the green card status, as well as greater training through increasing my educational achievements. This new season was a definite answer to prayer for me — to be in the position of a permanent resident in New York City. I knew that God was positioning me not only to improve my employment and professional training, but also to be able to minister in a greater way to those around me. Ultimately, He was planting me to bear more fruit for Him.

Chapter 7

Citizen of Heaven

...that having been justified by His grace
we should become heirs according to
the hope of eternal life. (Titus 3:7)

As a believer on a journey of faith with God, I can say from my experience that there is nothing like walking in the favor of God's grace. To know that we belong to Him, being justified by His grace and not by our merit, brings confidence in every situation that we don't need to be afraid because He can and will make a way for us. Though we live and walk in the midst of the circumstances of this life, God's life and presence within our lives bring to those same circumstances a higher authority that supersedes any earthly situations or challenges.

In my particular story, the miracle of receiving my permanent residency in the United States of America was not the only instance that God moved on my behalf regarding residency and citizenship. There was another situation that demonstrated that His favor in my life was greater than the temporary systems of this world.

A situation happened in my family that necessitated my traveling back to Trinidad for an extended visit. While there, I was living with the two children that I had borne with the second man in my life, and their grandmother. One day I was at home and I heard a knock on the door, I went to answer it. Standing in the doorway were two immigration officers asking to see me. Needless to say, I was quite surprised, when I discovered that my children's grandmother had attempted to get me deported.

Not wanting to make the situation any worse than it already was, I corporate with the immigration officers as they carried out their investigation of my status in Trinidad. At the immigration office, I was asked to show my passport, I told the Immigration officers upon my return to Trinidad my passport was stolen and I didn't make a report to the police. Without my passport, I couldn't prove I have my residency through my husband who is a Trinidadian citizen.

As I anticipated, the officers proceeded to tell me that I was an illegal immigrant in Trinidad. I now face a situation where I would be sent back to Saint Vincent and the Grenadines, though I had lived in Trinidad for many years previously. Back home, I would have to apply for a new passport and then come back to Trinidad to apply for my residency.

The challenge I had at that time was that. I didn't have the money to travel to Saint Vincent and the Grenadines to acquire a new passport. Then, at that very moment, God intervened. Something happened that I have not heard of in any other situation before or since that time: one of the men in the immigration department gave me a loan to buy my ticket to go to Saint Vincent and the Grenadines. I was shocked and amazed, and most certainly relieved, to hear that news! What the enemy meant for evil—even in that challenging situation—God turned around for good!

With the provision that was granted to me, I went back to my home country of Saint Vincent and the Grenadines. I hadn't seen my mother or other family members for a very long time. It was a strange feeling going back home after so much had happened in my life apart from my extended family, but I knew that God had a purpose in my visit. Later I would find out that it played a part in opening doors for me to minister to my family in powerful ways in the future.

On this particular trip, I stayed in Saint Vincent and the Grenadines just long enough to get my new passport. I took very little with me on that trip, but I did take something for my grandmother who was still alive. She was my dear grandmother who had raised me as a child, and she always would have a very special place in my heart. She was elated to see me, and though I stayed at my mother's home, I spent most of the time with my grandmother, who was very elderly by this time and lived in another town. She gave me so much love!

Seeing my grandmother was a bright spot on my trip, and it showed me how God was in control of my life to bring about His plans for me. I belonged to Him, and nothing in this world could change that truth. Having accomplished what I went to do, I went back to Trinidad to update my residency and to pay back the loan that had been granted to me.

Sometimes it can feel like my life is at the mercy of others' decisions, which may or may not be for my best interest. Through it all, however, I have come to realize that being a citizen of heaven is more powerful than any earthly passport! When we are citizens in God's Kingdom by His grace, His love, and His salvation, it sets our priorities in order when it comes to earthly citizenship and the affairs of this world. No matter which nation in which we may be official citizens, our status in that nation is merely temporary. It takes second place to our eternal, unchanging status in God's family.

Philippians 3:20-21 says:

For our citizenship is in heaven, from which we also eagerly wait for the Savior, the Lord Jesus Christ, who will transform our lowly body that it may be conformed to His glorious body, according to the working by which He is able even to subdue all things to Himself.

Our citizenship in heaven is a guarantee of the everlasting work that God desires to do in our hearts and lives. He is undeterred by any roadblock, "red tape", or governmental reality in this world. He is not hindered by the deep hurts and traumatic experiences that we may encounter in this life. He is not even thwarted by our personal failures and weaknesses. His purpose is forever set in place: it is to conform us to the character and person of Jesus Christ.

God's all-powerful ability is enough to overcome any obstacle that may stand in His way. Our part is simply to surrender to Him, to trust His plans, and to walk through the doors that He opens for us. One day the final door we walk through, as those saved by grace, will be the door through which He welcomes us into His heavenly Kingdom, saying, "Well done, good and faithful servant" (Matthew 25:21). What an amazing reality it is to be a citizen of heaven!

Chapter 8

My Children

But the mercy of the Lord is from ever-lasting to everlasting on those who fear Him, and His righteousness to children's children. (Psalm 103:17)

In the same way that I made a conscious effort to minister to Mrs. Melderson and other people in my life, I have always looked for opportunities to continue ministering to my children. As you can imagine, they are the most important people to me!

Sometimes I reach out to my children in ways of focused prayer and spiritual encouragement, and other times in more practical ways like giving advice or sending a special care package. In whatever way that I reach out to them, it comes from a heart that desires the best that God has for them. This is one of the greatest joys and passions in my life— "that my children walk in truth" (III John 1:4)!

Though I was able to see my children nearly every weekend when I first came to America, unfortunately, it was not always that easy afterwards to arrange.

In my first six years in the United States, I grew closer to my children because they would come to me on holidays and other special times when I was living in New York. But now that my children are grown and they are all living in different states except for one who still lives in New York. Sometimes they came to stay with me, other times I go to be with them. We talk and stay in touch, though I don't see them as often as I would like to due to the circumstances and the physical distance between us. We communicate on the phone when we can't see each other and we have become closer that way.

With my children being far away I looked for creative ways to connect with them. Sometimes I took a road trip via the bus just to be with them, which was a great blessing for me and also an opportunity for me to share the love of God with them in an intentional way.

I am so thankful that God is bigger than the challenges we face! There were times when we faced many challenges, but I know God is more powerful than those challenges and I trust Him daily to make a way for us to work out everything in our lives. God's assurance to me is that He is in control of my family is the only way I can make it through when it feels like my relationships with my children are not as close as I would hope for. Sometimes I ask God how He is going to work it out. He doesn't usually tell me everything He is about to do, but His grace and His assurance are enough in those moments.

I know that God will never leave us apart from His watchful care. I can even remember a time when one of my sons was seriously sick, and I prayed to God and he was healed! There have been other times when I have grown impatient, wanting God to answer in the way that I desire for my children when they are going through a season of difficulty. We don't know *how* God is going to answer, but we can be assured as His children that he always will hear our prayers and *will* answer us as our Father.

As a mother, I often feel it personally when my children are struggling in an area of their lives. One memorable example of this, that became a wonderful answer to prayer involved one of my sons. I had known that he and his family were getting very overweight because of their eating habits. So I asked God for wisdom to know what to do because I was worried about him and his family. God revealed a plan which I shared with them. To God be the Glory, today they are all in a much better place health-wise. Thank God all of my children are healthy and have rewarding careers.

I want to encourage you today that if you have children, those special ones in your life are your greatest mission field. Too often, we look for a glamorous calling in God that will take us to far-away lands to preach the gospel or to become well known for serving the Lord. Sometimes God does ask us to do those things, but I believe that He is looking for our daily obedience to Him to minister to our children's lives that He has entrusted to our care. Though it may go unseen this side of heaven, no spiritual exploits or numerous accomplishments will ever be greater than that!

Chapter 9

A Family Breakthrough

For all have sinned and fall short of the glory of God, being justified freely by His grace through the redemption that is in Christ Jesus. (Romans 3:23-24)

For me, living so far away from many of my family members has not been an easy path, because of how important my family is to me and how much I love them. As a believer in Jesus, I have for many years longed for the fullness of God's purpose to be realized in the lives of my immediate family members. Having experienced firsthand the power of God's love and redemption in my life, it can sometimes be difficult to not get ahead of God or to "help" make His wonderful plan come to pass for my family in my strength. But as I have learned in so many circumstances in my own life, God's timing and His ways are always best.

For the first time since the miracle that took place with the immigration office in Trinidad, I returned to Saint Vincent and the Grenadines in 2013 to spend time once again with my family. By this time my grandparents had died (the ones dear to my heart who had raised me), so on this particular trip, I went to spend some time with my mother and I focused on seeing her the most during the visit.

In those moments with my mother, I tried to talk to her and ask her many questions about her life, and one of these questions that I asked her was why she gave me away to my father when I was a child. She answered and said to me that it was because my father wanted me. But I said to her, "Mother, you are the one who made me and gave birth to me—I am your child! You weren't supposed to give me to my father!" I told her that she was the one who carried me for nine months until I was born, and it didn't make sense to give me away and not be more involved in my everyday life as a young child.

With that, she began to tell me the whole story of what was happening in our family during the period when I was born. She shared with me that she never was actually in love with my father, and how hard it was for her as a young mother to handle life's circumstances in those days, to which I could relate as a mother myself.

What I gathered from our conversation was that she gave me away because if she would have kept me, I would have reminded her of my father. So I asked her again to understand more fully, and we sat and talked for hours. We spoke about many memories and about many questions I had for my mother that I had never been able to ask her before.

For example, I asked my mother why when I was a young child, she would sometimes come to the town where I was living with my grandparents, but she never came to see me. She told me that she didn't come because she didn't want my stepmother to think that she was coming after my father. I shared with her honestly that this was a lame, unconvincing excuse because she and my father had known each other for many years and it would not have been plausible to assume that my mother would have intended any malice.

For the first two nights, I was there with my mother, we talked all night, coming to a greater understanding and closer relationship between the two of us. In talking about things that could have been very painful to discuss, God gave me the grace to show love towards my mother and to speak with her heart to heart, which brought significant healing to both of us.

As I visited with her at that time, and as we talked and tried to mend the relationship where there had been hurts in the past, I forgave my mother for everything that happened—because we all are human and we all make mistakes, because God's love is greater, and because I had made it through all those difficult times and more by the grace of God.

I believe that I came into this world for a reason and that everything happens for a reason. Whatever happens in life, it is my conviction that it can make you closer to God or make you more distant from God. The choice is ours. A lot of people say that I am very strong because of the things that I did to survive, but I know that it was only through the grace of God and not through my ability. These were things that I shared with my mother during my visit, conveying to her God's central role in my life.

I had a wonderful time with my brothers and sisters at that time in Saint Vincent and the Grenadines, and I have continued to feel a part of the family throughout the past and to this very day. Every time I would see them, however, I would look for opportunities to talk to them about God.

Perhaps the greatest example of this is my late sister, who passed away just a few years ago. My sister was not a Christian, and I went to her house to try to share with her about my faith. When I did so, I also talked to her about her eating habits, because she was a diabetic and I was concerned for her the same way I was concerned about my mother and other family members who struggled with the same condition.

Because I believe in healthy eating, it was natural for me to bring up this subject while I was sharing with my sister. I told her that because she was a diabetic, she had to especially watch how she ate. I shared with her that she needed to stop eating only white rice and to start eating a lot of other healthier foods instead, and I gave her some ideas on how to reduce the sugar in her diet. My sister didn't respond well, however. She told me that I was trying to be a doctor in her life and she didn't want to listen to me. When I called her later, she still was not open to what I was saying to her and was speaking very rough to me.

My sister's health got progressively worse because of diabetes and because she did not want to change her eating habits. Her two kidneys began to fail, and she was in a very poor condition. I told my sister that God had sent me to talk to her for a reason so that she could live because the Bible said that we shall live and not die, and declared the works of the Lord (Psalm 118:17). But my words seemed to only fall to the ground.

As it turned out, I talked to both my mother and my sister about similar things, but only my mother listened to me. She felt that I was a messenger bringing her the truth of God. My sister who did not listen eventually she died from the complications of diabetes and kidney failure.

But God is a God of redemption! Just when I thought all was lost, God brought about a powerful breakthrough in our family.

In 2016, my children promised to buy me a ticket to travel to Saint Vincent and the Grenadines for Christmas. But when it came time to buy the ticket, it was quite expensive and they couldn't purchase it. I had hoped very much to be able to go to see my sister one more time because of her ailing condition, I became very disappointed when it looked like I wouldn't be able to get the ticket. The director at my job knew, that I was sad about not being able to go to visit my sister. So she made it possible for me to borrow $2,000 from my job so that I could go and visit my family in Saint Vincent and the Grenadines and also take Christmas gifts for them. So because of this, I was able to see all my family, including my mother, and especially my very sick sister. I knew that God had made a way for me to secure the flight and was trusting that He would also make a way for His message to get through to my sister.

When I arrived to see my family, I went to visit my sister, and I was so elated and thankful that I was able to finally come to see her again after my visit three years earlier. This time when I saw her, she felt sorry because she knew then that I had given her good advice when we had seen each other last. I talked with her every day on that visit—we talked and talked for hours, and she even wanted me to come to her house and sleep there.

I talked to her about God and I didn't hold anything back. I preached the word to her, knowing that this probably would be the last opportunity I would have to reach out to her. I let her know that Jesus Christ died for each one of us and that He came to heal us from every curse and every kind of sickness, and so I prayed for healing for her. But I prayed that if it was God's will to heal her, that He would heal her; and if it was His will to take her, that He would take her, as Scripture says, "to be absent from the body and to be present with the Lord" (II Corinthians 5:8).

I cried when I shared openly with her, and I also brought her special gifts to show her God's kindness and the love of Jesus. As I prayed with her, at that moment her heart was softened, and I know that my sister accepted Jesus Christ to be her personal Lord and Savior. And because of that amazing day of God's miraculous salvation, I know that my sister went to meet with the Lord. Praise God for His saving love!

On that trip in 2016, I was so thankful to be able to spend time with my mother and my relatives, and yet it was also a sad and bittersweet time because I got to see everyone but it was also the last time I was able to see my sister before she died. Even though my sister and I were not very close before that visit (because we were not raised together), I found that God knit our hearts together in a new way through that very special time that I spent with her. Family is very important, and this was certainly the case for me in that season, even in ways that I did not expect: now my sister miraculously had also become my sister in Christ.

Though it was hard for me after my sister passed away and I missed her, I knew that she had gone to meet with the Lord. So I rested in the encouragement from God that my sister had gone to be with Him in heaven, where there is no sickness or pain, but only joy.

The story of my interactions with my sister taught me how important it is to meet people in their hard times, right where they are, with compassion and with the love of God, because it is a unique and powerful opportunity for them to find Him and to see Him in a personal, life-changing way.

The story of how God saved my sister also showed me so clearly that no one is beyond the reach of our God! It doesn't matter what you have done in your past; if you come to God and confess your need for Him, and simply receive what His Son Jesus Christ has done on the cross for you, today you can know His salvation. Have you received Him as Savior? Do you know Him personally today? If you do not yet, or if you have strayed from Him, today is the day that you can meet Him in a real way for the first time. Don't miss this powerful moment as He is calling your name. I want to invite you to pray this prayer with me right now:

Heavenly Father, I confess that I am a sinner in need of Your amazing grace. Thank You that You sent Your Son Jesus Christ to take the penalty for all the things that I have done wrong. Forgive me for where I have turned my back on You and lived for myself instead. Today I turn to You with my whole heart. I believe that You alone are the Way, the Truth, and the Life (John 14:6). Save me now and make me Your child. I give my life to You now and forever. In Jesus' Name, Amen.

If you just prayed that prayer from your heart, angels in heaven are rejoicing that you have come home to your Heavenly Father! Begin now to seek out others who can encourage you in your faith, and begin reading the Bible to allow God's Word to find its place in your heart. In the same measure to which my family members and I have experienced this acceptance from God, you are now part of God's family! "But as many as received Him, to them He gave the right to become children of God, to those who believe in His name" (John 1:12).

Chapter 10

In Every Season

*Let your speech always be with grace,
seasoned with salt, that you may know
how you ought to answer each one.*
(Colossians 4:6)

A remarkable thing happens when any person from any walk of life submits their self to God's authority and guidance: that person begins to walk through life by the daily leading of the Holy Spirit. Above all, one characteristic that is always present in someone who has truly encountered Jesus Christ is a love for others that is not dependent on circumstances. It is a supernatural occurrence in that person's heart to change him or her from being ungrateful for God's blessings to being contagiously thankful for the love of God experienced within.

As I live my life serving God each day, I have seen so many lives touched by God's presence and love. If I were to share all the miracles that I have seen God perform, I would feel like the Apostle John when he said that the whole world could not contain the books that could be written about what Jesus has done (John 21:25).

In the many different seasons of life, I have learned to always be ready for however and wherever God wants to use me. Paul said it this way in his scriptural charge to Timothy: "Preach the word! Be ready in season and out of season..." (II Timothy 4:2). Being ready "in season and out" is not easy and I am far from perfect in it. But I know that this is the lifestyle to which God has called me. And it is never boring!

Recently I worked on the weekends as a caregiver for a patient, as I often do with people whom God brings in my path, I talked to her about my relationship with God. Many times I would sit with her and talk to her about God, and I would tell her how much God loves her. I often would give her a testimony so that she could hear what God has done in my life and how He opened doors for me.

When she told me she was so glad I was there with her, I shared with her that God opened the door for this job so that I could take care of her. She grew to appreciate my care.

One time this particular patient was sick, and I took her to the bathroom where she slumped over in pain, and she vomited. The choking and fainting that she exhibited seemed to indicate that something may have happened with her heart. So I called 911, and when they came they confirmed that she was having a heart attack. She, like others I have cared for, has grown to love me because I am familiar with what to do in these types of situations, and I have a heart to truly care for people. Because I am kind toward my patients, they usually understand that I mean well when I speak with them about spiritual things.

When this lady was sick in the hospital, I laid my hands on her and prayed for her to get well and that she would be able to go back to her home once again. The doctors had done some blood work, and if the blood work came back positive she would have to stay in the hospital, but if it came back negative she would be able to go home. At this time in her life, she was in her nineties and wanted to be in her own house.

After we prayed, the blood works came back negative and she was able to go back home. So we went home together and we continued to pray when God made it possible to do so. I persisted in looking for more opportunities to reach out to her and prayed for the access to speak God's love into her life.

As I did so, she would ask me to only pray silently when I asked to talk to her about God. One day she even said she didn't want to hear about God at all. When she had a lot of discomfort and was not feeling well, she would often blame God for the pain she felt in her body and for her problems, and she seemed to be growing bitter against Him. I would try to talk to her, telling her that Jesus Christ came and died for us and that through His blood we receive God's love and salvation. Occasionally when she was warmer towards the idea, she would listen to me pray.

Sometimes when I am working in different places I like to play Christian music on my phone, but she would tell me that she didn't want songs like that playing in her house. So I would respect her wishes about her home, but I would continue to look for ways to share with her how much God loves her. She would sometimes listen, but these days it is getting difficult to share with her, as she tends to not be easily receptive.

She had a total of three aides: besides me, and no one talked with her about God during the week (I am only there on the weekends). I prayed she accepted Christ in her life before she breathed her last breath on this earth. I prayed for her faithfully and I talked with her, and when I told her God loved her and how wonderful He is, she said, "Yes!" But there have been times when I wanted to pray with her and she responded that she doesn't believe that God exists. So I trust that God has sent me to bless her life and that everything has to be in God's time and not my own. Some of God's miracles, I have learned, happened step by step—but they are miracles nonetheless.

On one weekend recently, I worked on Saturday night and Sunday. On weekends like this, I usually take Saturday to devote as my day set apart for God, going to church and spending the rest of the day with Him. The lady I was caring for had an accident in which she fell out of her wheelchair, broke her hip, and had to go back to the hospital.

While she was in the hospital, I called and asked how she was doing as she had just had surgery, afterwards, I went to see her in her hospital and I prayed for her in person. She was ninety-four years old, and I prayed for her that she would be able to continue with her normal life as she did before the surgery, and not only that but also that she would come out of it stronger and fully healed.

The doctors put screws in her hip, and eventually, after an initial recovery, they sent her home. I pray for her continually that she will be able to walk again and overcome this trial. She is an independent person who enjoys her autonomy, and these things are very important to her. It may seem like just a simple matter, but I prayed that she would at least be able to walk to the bathroom on her own, as it would make all the difference for her.

I still also pray for her that one day, in a moment, she would respond to God's calling out to her and accept Jesus Christ as her Savior. In my conversations with her, I try to steer her in that direction, asking her questions that will lead her closer to Jesus. I continued to work with her until she dies in 2018.

Because I have intentionally made myself available to be used by God, it is not unusual for me that I have distinct opportunities to reach out to strangers as I am going about my daily life. There are a lot of people like this whom I have the opportunity to pray for, and God often touches their lives in special ways through these instances.

One such occurrence took place one day as I was traveling on the ferry in New York City. I met a certain man there who asked me if I would pray for him, as he said that he saw something in me that made him feel that I could pray. So I prayed for him, his job and other things that were on his heart. And God ministered to him in a unique way at that time.

I know God is working in me through His Holy Spirit! My friends will call me sometimes and share something they are about to do, and I may tell them that I don't think it's a good idea, or that I don't think God will like it. In any case, I have prophesied many things into people's lives that have come to pass, and many times they will ask me what I think about something because they believe that God speaks through me.

I believe that there are many gifts that God has placed within me (and also in you) that we need to give birth too. I don't know how everything will look when it appears, or what timing these things will all happen, but I do know that God made me for this type of ministry to others and that He wants me to live my life for Him *on purpose*, ministering to those around me. As I make myself available I know I need to just let go and let God work!

I know that I am nothing in this world without God, and ultimately all these things are His work and not my own. In John 15:5, Jesus says, "…without Me you can do nothing", and I know experientially that this is completely true. There are times in my life that I can't even physically walk without God, so I trust Him to be the center of my life in everything I do. In everything that I do, as much as I possibly can, I pray and ask God to have His way in it.

Sometimes I might have a problem or something that I want to do, and I will ask God, "God, is it all right to do this?" I have come to see and to believe that if something is God's will, then it eventually is going to work out. And if it's not His will, then it won't come to pass—it just slowly fades away, disappears. God is my all; He is my everything, and without Him, I am nothing in this world.

It is God's love and ultimate sacrifice for us all that allows me to make sacrifices of my own to bless others. For instance, I had a situation recently at my house, where I rented out my bedroom to a couple who didn't have anywhere to live when they got married. I decided

I would rent them my bedroom because I felt that if they were staying in my living room they would not have enough privacy to feel at home. So I moved out of my bedroom and was staying in the living room instead so that they could use my bedroom. However, the situation didn't work out.

But do you know how I look at this situation? I look at how Jesus Christ came into this world, and how He gave up His home in glory, in heaven, with the Father. He gave up His very life for us! So when I think that giving up my bedroom—my personal comfort zone—for another person, I just think about how Jesus gave up His life for me. It doesn't mean that there is no struggle, but it does mean that there is strength to overcome it.

A lot of people would find me to be foolish for doing something like that, or others would think that I am stupid, but I lived like this because I knew that God wanted me to live this way in my house for that season. This for me is the bottom line. It might cause many problems that I have to face—and I have gone through a lot of issues with the people who stayed with me—but I know that when I look back, they are going to be a blessing to me because I am walking in obedience to God.

Like anyone, sometimes I face difficulties in my life, and during those times I often call out to God and I say, "God, help me!" And He is so good, so marvelous! He supplies every need that I have. Sometimes when I haven't had any money, the Spirit of God has told me to go to specific places where He supplies the need. There was one such day when I didn't have any money, and the Spirit of God told me to go somewhere—to a specific place. And when I went, I met my friends there, and everybody gave me money! So God has been abundantly good to me, in more ways than I can even describe. I don't know what I would do without God!

I have found in many circumstances that I may want things one way, but God wants it another way. I have faced this reality many times! The comfort we can find as believers in the midst of these challenges is that in the end, everything really *will* work out for our good because God has promised to bless us. Though it may not always seem like it, that is where we learn to trust Him.

Because I have learned to trust God, I see Him at work now more and more in our family. Recently I went to a party also attended by my ex-husband and sister-in-law. I was with everyone there, and it was a really wonderful time! Even when someone tried to bring up some painful things from the past, I was able to tell them, "The past is over and it's gone! Today we live for today!" We don't know what tomorrow may bring, so we must focus on enjoying today and being thankful for all the blessings God gives to us. Having seen God's miracles in so many ways, now I just want to praise and thank God for all He has done for me!

Without a doubt, God has healed me from a lot of pain through the years as I have given my life to following Him. In my relationships and life circumstances, I have been through many challenges, and I have needed Him to work inside my heart. I would often say to God, "Even with all the things I have gone through, I just cannot hold on to grudges or hold on to hate!" If someone would do something hurtful to me, I would usually not do anything to address it with that person—I would simply move on in God's grace and strength. And people will often say to me, "But why do you just move on? How can you just let things go like that?" My reply to them is that God came to us in Jesus Christ, and forgave me so that I can forgive others!

As I reflect on all that God has brought me through, in Saint Vincent and the Grenadines, in Trinidad, and now in America, this is the message that God has given me in my life to share with others—that God's grace is enough. He is the God of salvation and the God who gives the miracle of new life, and His blessings are available to anyone who will call on His name from a sincere heart. Why would I not want to share that with those around me? I don't know what the future holds for me, but I know that I must be ready in season and out of season to share His love, and I challenge you to do the same. You never know how He might use you— He is the God of miracles!

A Miracle Book

Thank you for allowing me to share with you the story of God's grace in my life. I hope that you have been blessed and encouraged by it! The story of this book being created is a miracle in itself. I never aspired to write a book of my own, but God had other plans for me, as I have seen Him do many times in my life.

About a year ago, I went to my bishop after he had exhorted us in the congregation to give a sacrificial offering. He was about to travel to Israel carrying our prayer requests with him, to pray over the prayer needs and requests. As I prayed, I felt God leading me to give an offering, and I did what God said to do and gave the amount that I heard Him leading me to give. At that moment, the prayer requests that I submitted were that I needed a husband, and also that I needed my life story changed by the Lord.

Before that time, I had been praying often, "God, I need my life changed… I need my story changed!" And in that split-second, as I prayed those words again, the Spirit of God stirred in me to write a book—the one that you now hold in your hands. I felt that God was telling me that taking this step would change my story. He spoke to me that I should testify about what He had done in my life, and also to prophesy what I believed He would do in my life in the future as I surrendered my story to Him.

I shared these impressions with my bishop, telling him about the book and about the sacrificial offering I had made. Because he is a kind man who shows a personal interest in others' lives, I was able to share with him about the monetary gift and also about the desire God had put within me to start writing. He asked me how many chapters I planned to write and other details about the project because he is the type of person who will help in any way he can, especially when he sees someone who is stepping out in faith and trusting God. He is a leader who wants the best for his "flock" and to see them prosper in every area and make their lives even better. So he was extremely glad about my idea and about what God had spoken to me, and he said that if I needed assistance writing the book, he would help to find people to write it with me. I told him that God provided everything and that the book was already in the making.

Both in this book project and other parts of my life, something God is teaching me is that I need to have more patience, because I can get overwhelmed at times. God is telling me, "My daughter, cast all your cares upon Me, for I care for you" (I Peter 5:7). I am finding now in my daily life that I just need to find the Word, to begin to absorb the truth of the Scriptures, and to let God work *for* me, on my behalf. God's Word is life!

In the book of Ezekiel, there is a place where Ezekiel took the Word of God and he ate it, and it became nourishment like vitamins to his body. If God's Word can do that for him, it can do the same for you and me! A significant part of my desire in writing this book was to point everyone who reads it to God's eternal words that are nourishment and strength to each of us.

I know deep inside me that God is *real*. Sometimes I go to my house, and I take time to just thank God and to praise Him because He wants us to do this in every situation—in good times and bad times. Just as the Bible says:

I will bless the Lord at all times; His praise shall continually be in my mouth. My soul shall make its boast in the Lord; the humble shall hear of it and be glad. Oh, magnify the Lord with me, and let us exalt His name together. I sought the Lord, and He heard me and delivered me from all my fears. (Psalm 34:1-4)

Because He is God and will always be God, He has to be the center of everything. As we take the step of obedience to praise God, even when we don't understand His timing, He begins to use our lives to minister to others so that they can come to Him also and exalt His name with us. That is the amazing God of grace that we serve!

Often when I go to my job, I put on some praise music using my radio, and that way I can praise God while I work. One day recently, as I was working on the book project in addition to the jobs that I already have, I said, "God, I surrender my all to You. I am tired of trying to do it by myself, in my strength. I cannot do it by myself—I need You! And I commit everything I have to You today." And I promised Him that I was going to try not to worry, and to commit everything into His hands and to allow Him to take charge. From that moment forward, this is exactly what He has done.

This book and the testimonies I included in it are ultimately not about me! Instead, everything I have written is about what the Spirit of God can do. And if God can do *anything*, He will make *everything* work out the way it is supposed to be—in His timing and not my timing, just as He has done with this book. Other years I have been too busy to undertake a project like this, but this year, everything came to pass and in the right timing.

Even including the details of how to pay for the project, I was sitting down one day, and the Spirit of God said, "Call the insurance!" I had just been praying about how to get the book written, and I called my insurance company and they told me I would be able to receive just the amount of money that I needed to begin the project. So God always does things in *His* timing.

Similarly, when I call my children, I pray for them and trust God that everything is going to work out in all our lives according to God's plan for us. And so I share with you today: trust God! Trust His ways! Trust His timing! Maybe someday you will also write a book of what He has done in your life. But whatever the case may be for you, use your story to praise the God who can do anything, and I know you will find that many will come to know Him and praise Him because of what He has done in your life. May God bless you as you make yourself available to what His miracle-working power will do in you and through you!

Ever thankful for His grace,
Elma Rivers

Words from Scripture to Memorize, Trust and Obey

Throughout my journey, the Bible has given me strength, hope, assurance, and confidence to face every trial in life. I have often shared these verses with others in my church, among my family and friends, as well as with those I have cared for and worked with. I encourage you to use God's word to strengthen your spirit and to share with others.

To me, who am less than the least of all the saints, this grace was given, that I should preach... the unsearchable riches of Christ... (Ephesians 3:20)

But by the grace of God, I am what I am, and His grace toward me was not in vain, but I labored more abundantly than they all, yet not I, but the grace of God which was with me. (I Corinthians 15:10)

For by grace you have been saved through faith, and that not of yourselves; it is the gift of God, not of works, lest anyone should boast. (Ephesians 2:8-9)

Let us then approach God's throne of grace with confidence, so that we may receive mercy and find grace to help us in our time of need. (Hebrews 4:16, NIV)

And we know that in all things God works for the good of those who love Him, who have been called according to His purpose. (Romans 8:28 NIV)

And of His fullness we have all received, and grace for grace. (John 1:16)

As each one has received a gift, minister it to one another, as good stewards of the manifold grace of God. (I Peter 4:10)

By the grace God has given me, I laid a foundation... (I Corinthians 3:10)

...that having been justified by His grace we should become heirs according to the hope of eternal life. (Titus 3:7)

For our citizenship is in heaven, from which we also eagerly wait for the Savior, the Lord Jesus Christ, who will transform our lowly body that it may be conformed to His glorious body, according to the working by which He is able even to subdue all things to Himself. (Philippians 3:20-21

But the mercy of the Lord is from everlasting to everlasting on those who fear Him, and His righteousness to children's children. (Psalm 103:17)

For all have sinned and fall short of the glory of God, being justified freely by His grace through the redemption that is in Christ Jesus. (Romans 3:23-24)

But as many as received Him, to them He gave the right to become children of God, to those who believe in His name. (John 1:12)

Let your speech always be with grace, seasoned with salt, that you may know how you ought to answer each one. (Colossians 4:6)

I will bless the Lord at all times; His praise shall continually be in my mouth. My soul shall make its boast in the Lord; the humble shall hear of it and be glad. Oh, magnify the Lord with me, and let us exalt His name together. I sought the Lord, and He heard me, and delivered me from all my fears. (Psalm 34:1-4)

I invite you to pray this prayer:

Heavenly Father, I confess that I am a sinner in need of Your amazing grace. Thank You that You sent Your Son Jesus Christ to take the penalty for all the things that I have done wrong. Forgive me for where I have turned my back on You and lived for myself instead. Today I turn to You with my whole heart. I believe that You alone are the Way, the Truth, and the Life (John 14:6). Save me now and make me Your child. I give my life to You now and forever. In Jesus' Name, Amen.

9 781545 668856